Phone Ringing
in a Dark House

Books by Rolly Kent

Poetry
The Wreck in Post Office Canyon
Spirit, Hurry
Phone Ringing in a Dark House

Nonfiction
Queen of Dreams (with Heather Valencia)

Collections
Southside: 21 Poems by Children from Tucson's Southside (editor)
Willa & Marie: Poems from a Nursing Home (editor, with Susan North)

Phone Ringing in a Dark House

Rolly Kent

Carnegie Mellon University Press
Pittsburgh 2023

Acknowledgments

Grateful acknowledgment is given to the following magazines in whose pages these poems first appeared:

American Poetry Review: "World War II"
BoomerLitMag: "The Hammock," "Owl"
Comstock Review: "Kindness" (as "Steak or Potato"), "In Scorpion Time" (as "The Sweetest Forgiveness")
I-70 Review: "Two Cherries," "When All the Storms Were Named after Women" (as "Stamps")
Louisville Review: "Rhode Island," "My Parents in the City of Light," "Could a Man Be a Snake?"
Under a Warm Green Linden: "In the Fifties"
Volume: "My Dog the Artist," "The Old Songs"

Book design by Jen Bortner

Library of Congress Control Number 2023933224
ISBN 978-0-88748-693-7
Printed and bound in the United States of America

10 9 8 7 6 5 4 3 2 1

for Miranda

&

in memory of my parents

Contents

I

II

III

Water

Around five-thirty in the morning
two ravens are prattling back and forth.
I'd rather not listen, but when they start
saying *Water Water Water,* I get out of bed—
what kind of ravens are these? I watch them
sail across the pale dawn then fly
back and forth from the ponderosa pine
on Briarcliff, to the eucalyptus
on Tuxedo, then back and forth again,
like reference librarians checking one
source against another, assessing the facts,
nodding their heads until the air itself
seems smitten with *Water.* By nature I'm
a doubter; I lie back down, troubled.
Is water the answer to everything?
What is the answer to water? Is it
the shore? Or is water the answer to water?
But then a third raven gets involved
and the three of them fly to some
houses in the canyon where the sun
has still not come and the people there have
questions that are the most human questions
ever, and those birds answer them
perfectly. They call back and forth; then
the sound grows faint. And yet when I hear it
repeated from far away, what they
are saying seems so clear, even obvious.

A Summer's Night in the Forties

Up on the hill with the high palm trees:
two stars, quite bright, rising as a pair
above the roofs and wavering fronds,
setting out on their nightly cross.

As a boy I loved stars and their loyalty
to the night, I loved that their names—
Cassiopeia, Andromeda, Lyra, Orion—
were songs in a future heaven.

Now that I know what we see is not
the stars themselves but the light each one
sheds as it travels farther from itself,
I love them even more for where they've been.

That summer's night when I wished upon them—
was that boy really me standing beneath hills
and trees and rooftops looking up? What was it
I wished, oh wish that has carried me here?

Two stars, quite bright, rising, pausing from
their travels above me. For all the stars
I would ever see and all those I would not,
they answered with what any star wants for itself:

Live, said the first one, *Live again*, said the other.

Phone Ringing in a Dark House

Ten steps farther down the road we stop again,
by a fence this time, when a phone inside
a dark house rings. I turn and listen.

Phineas swishes the dirt with his tail
and pushes his sweet old face against my leg.
He wants me to sing like Wilson Pickett:

What's my number? Then he'll sing: *six-three-four-five-
seven-eight-nine.* And I'll go: *That's my number.*
And he'll go: *six-three-four-five-seven-eight-nine.*

He's crazy about that chorus, though on
the high notes he struggles. No matter. We're still
believers in each other and our own private lines.

Just past the foot bridge he stops again, looks
across the river above the cottonwoods as if
he sees Noah there pronouncing the name of this

moment. He turns around and says, *Remember
to breathe.* Of course, I reply. *And,* he adds,
remember rock 'n' roll, and pasta Bolognese, and

the phone nobody answered, and symmetry—and,
I interrupt, you're telling me this why?
Just try to be where you're needed most.

That's my motto. He stares into the sky.
Life! he announces. *Life is never through.*
Isn't it? I ask him. Doesn't it have to be?

Maybe, he admits. *But love what you know,*
I hear him say over and over until it sounds
the same as love what you do not know.

In Scorpion Time

Ever since in deep bright moonlight
I rolled over in bed onto the scorpion,
I've never again killed one, whether they
come out of the walls and climb like
the constellation part way up the cool
plaster sky, or walk across the tile
like tired fathers with their shoes unlaced.
They look and are ancient, as if they
no longer need to eat. Scorpio is their clock:
From the spring when he tracks down Orion
until his tail dips in October below
the old Yaqui mountains, all between
is their season, and in some way mine.

Right now there is one in a jelly glass
by the garage window. I have done this
many times: Cover him with the jar
as if you want to listen in to
a conversation on the other side, then
slide a stiff paper between jar and wall,
careful not to snag a pincer or a foot.
He cocks his tail and widens his arms,
scurries nowhere on the glass and quits.
Thus should all, he says, *retire from illusion.*

When I got stung, his ancestor showed me
the real illusory me, the big baby
flying through the darkness, as if I could
outrun venom. For within one minute
my left leg was about to explode like

an ancho chile on the fire. Help me,
I cried to my sleeping wife, do something!
Get some tenderizer, get the ammonia!
I did not die; I settled for a bag
of ice. For hours an electric surge
came and went, yet I could hardly blame
The Ancestor: I hurt him; he lashed out.

But even if he had wailed at the top of
his eight tiny lungs my fate was to
sleep until he struck. He was approximately
one and three-quarters inches long; perhaps
in scorpion time he was just a boy.
I sat with my ice in the dark by the bed.
In death he looked like a crucifix
with two broken arms. *Stay with me,* his little
ghost implored. So I pinned his body above
my pillow. But someone, oh someone with
a lot of nerve took him down from the wall.
She did not see how the sting had changed me.

Bougainvillea

because they ask nothing from the living,
it's as if they aren't dead
—Nâzim Hikmet

The bougainvillea are falling one by one
from their festival wall of red and gold,

some open, some broken, like lockets without
any faces inside. I look back to the book

at hand, Hikmet's poems, a pink petal
marking something I read once and wanted to

return to, but didn't: "Conversation with
Dead Nezval." Turning to those pages I see

that petal, so imperfectly preserved, has
donated some of its blood to Hikmet's words

for his friend, Vítězslav Nezval, leaving
the kind of smudge a highlighter makes,

or the smear of a pastel kiss, residues
of study and farewell bougainvillea

would make if it could speak. And where better
for a flower to die than pressed between

lines of a poem, kept in there not for beauty,
which is plentiful, but for the bravery

one needs reminding of in order to let beauty go.
Just as I'm about to return it to the page

with dead Nezval, the rain promised for weeks
at last arrives, scattering red and gold hearts

across the deck. For a while they color the wood
where it is wet, but the stain does not sink deep.

I add to them this one I was saving.
It releases the rest of its crimson, cryptic

ink that will finally be spent in nature
where there is no reminder and no regret.

White Ducks

White ducks headed towards the city
on a tandem flatbed, three or four ducks
to a cage, the cages crated in rows five
across and eight high and maybe forty
cages long—say it's one thousand six
hundred ducks hurtling along with their backs
turned to the highway and a few whose wings,
as I do the math, blow up over their heads
from the velocity of life which they
cannot stop, and the weird flapping disturbs
some of their cage-mates who open an eye
and shut it and then open it as they are
struck by the errant wings of their friend who is
powerless to help himself, and then they look out,
like old people on the deck of a ship
bound for distant ports, a retirement cruise
or journey to the homeland, and they see
only water, the days and nights are
water, all the fish, the plankton and coral,
the cruisers, the dinghies—at such speed it's
all water. The red bill, the black bill, the yellow,
the orange bills, some on one foot, some
crouched low. One thousand six hundred ducks
traveling from the country where they were born.

Rhode Island

Andy's Poem

We're standing like men at their urinals
should, keeping porcelain between us,
when Andy announces his prostate's
the size of Rhode Island. Before I can boast
mine is Delaware, a youth slides into
the empty stall, smug as the kid who ditched
U.S. Geography. We won't quiz him.
What states he doesn't know will still be there
to greet him: Some days it will be Connecticut
with its throbbing rivers, some days big-bellied
Ohio, or Wyoming with its yawning, yellow
plains. Young man, welcome! Stand with us
shoulder to shoulder, slacker and the slacked,
our backs against the world! Join us, unafraid
to gaze into the white and cherry-scented
abyss or upwards where the cracks in heaven are
and God leaked into the ceiling. For men never
know where divinity may find them. Be ready,
one hand free on your hip. But humble,
mindful to zip, and when finished, think of
Rhode Island ceaselessly pounded by ocean,
like the self, ever renewing, onward
flowing towards Providence, its capital.

In the Fifties

In traffic a young woman on a rented
bike catches up, overtakes, falls back
as my taxi moves along one of the streets

in the Fifties, her bike passing the cab,
the cab passing the bike until a stretch
when we ride at the same pace, Youth and Age

side by side, Age seeing the glow of sweat
on her upper lip, Youth squinting at
a cab carrying its someone-or-other,

hardly even a person, overwritten
as I must look by reflections of buildings
and the new sky, or, as she glances at

the tinted glass, by the inflection of
her own face, her worker's coveralls,
the star points of the city in which I am

a small fossil in the strata of other times,
the other Fifties when I saw in *Life*
magazine this same girl interrupting

the great fields of boyhood not with
rockets or lies about the failed Russian
harvest—instead, Khrushchev showed her off

in a long line of blond girls waving
Soviet flags. I found her face and tore out
the page; now here she is again, pedaling

beside me on Fifty-Third Street where
her golden hair is shining, accidental and
intimate, like the wheat crop that never was.

When All the Storms Were Named
after Women

Hurricane Connie swept into the softness
of New Jersey at a hundred miles an hour
and headed straight for the candle I'd left
burning by my bed. She hurled the window wide
and threw the fire onto my album
of stamps, waking me just enough to hear
her laugh, "*Haha oh foolish boy!*" First flames
enthralled my buffalos, then seized my
zeppelins, my rare Columbus upon
a horse, the flags of the lost, Freedom's
pretty blue face—everything flashed and burned.
Enter my father crying, "*Holy holy Hell!*"
He slammed the window shut, ran for water
and dowsed the last fizzlings of the fire
that took commemoration wherever
fire takes such things, leaving behind
the smell of smoke and the usual question:
What in the world had I been thinking? Yet,
when morning came my father's only words
were, "Go get some rakes." So I did, while he
untangled an extension cord, plugged in
the radio, and set it on the stoop. Together
we walked out into the storm's debris
and started to rake. Grass bristled with sparks
of sunshine. The Giants were playing
the Pirates in Pittsburgh, a double-header,
important games. "Go turn it up," Dad said.

World War II

My father would not talk about the war.
But there was a story my mother liked to tell.
They were stationed with the Air Corps,
Mother pregnant. One day, as she napped
on the couch and the makeshift fan droned on
and on like Kansas, my father sneaked off
Day Duty into the married barracks.
He unholstered his service pistol and
chilled the barrel with ice. Then, the way
my mother told it, my father crossed the floor
on tiptoe and lifted her blouse. She was
dreaming something that made her smile
when against her exposed belly she felt
the cold .45. At first she was
merely startled; but when she saw him
double up with laughter she yelled, *What is
wrong with you? It's not funny, Mr. Smart!*
She'd end her tale with a laugh that sounded
the way he laughed when he could no longer
hide his mirth. But that's not what vexed me—
the war was over before I was conceived.
Only after Dad died did I ask if she had
confused the details or made them up, because
how could I have been born in wartime?
"You?" my mother said. "It wasn't about you."
A brother before me had briefly lived.
She'd kept the truth like a gun concealed
in the world that failed her. "There," she said.
"Is that enough history for you?"

Kindness

After Bobby Belmondo beat me up,
I watched the night as it mixed with my blood
and I thought how black the final black will be
when I expire from something more, or less,
grievous than the swollen left eye and
bloody nose Bobby gave me. It was a brief
thought because as I swooned between earth
and heaven Bobby pulled me upright. "You're
scaring me, kid," he said and he and Ralph,
the heavyweight, walked me gently over to
the boarded up Lackawanna freight
station where they proceeded to allay
their own fear of death by giving me a
boxing clinic on how, with my gangly reach,
I should have jabbed and hit more. My defeat
had made them kind. I even got a ride
in the maroon Mercury coupé. "You're
alright, kid," Bobby said. I got out,
stood there, dazed by the mystery of loss.
The glasspack muffler rumbled down the hill,
far into the night that went on endlessly
and everywhere. Then I entered the house.

My father, bless him, as if he had waited
fifteen years to be of some genuine
assistance to his son, looked at my face
and saw his moment had come. He went
down on one knee to reach into the back
of the freezer where he had set aside
a misshapen, crystalized steak no

thicker than a slice of pumpernickel.
My mother was aghast: "Who did this?" she
demanded. My father only shrugged as he
handed off the frosty steak, motioning
to place it on my face, which got my mother
insisting it would be better to treat
my eye, now swollen completely shut, with
a cut potato. "You want to draw
infection, not add to it with a piece
of meat. God only knows where it came from."
My father smiled wanly, knowing of the
many things he could say, "Babe, it's frozen,"
was correct. He gestured again to hold
the steak on my face. They kept arguing
which was better, steak or potato. "Look,"
Dad said, "we won't always be here, so he
needs to learn to take care of things himself."
I went to my room and slept with the steak
on my eye. I took care of things because
we won't always be here, but seen from
memory it seems we always will.

What Minnie Would Want

As she lay in hospice the few hours
before she would die, I came to Minnie's bed
and told her I loved her, we all loved her,

and now she could go. But she was in
a cocoon not even the tv could
penetrate, not even the score sheet of

the Mets game, not even a game of poker.
Her glasses were gone, and those eyes that had
played a hundred thousand tiles of mahjongg

were closed for good. No more food, no more juice.
I touched her forehead as you would a child's.
She was peaceful, and in no hurry, so

I said those things you make up when
the conversation that is life goes quiet
and there is really nothing more to say.

For some reason, my last words to Minnie
were amongst the stupidest I ever spoke.
Don't come back, I said in her ear. But I

didn't mean it like it sounds. I meant, Be free.
You had one hard life; why have another?
As soon as I said it I knew Minnie

would want to come back. That would be
Minnie's way. *What a dumb idea*, she'd say.
Of course life is hard, what did you think? Life

is life. Even a baby knows this is
where to be. "Don't come back?" I'm just
going to forget you ever said that.

Don's Song

The money was gone; he moved to a cabin
of friends of a friend. Taught a few classes
and one Sunday afternoon after tidying up,
walked into the steep spruce and redwood forest,
leaving his medical bracelet behind.
This troubled those who came knocking.
A search party combed the woods but
by then each clue belonged to Don's song.
What his body needed was to be a note
in the song, to lie down with one ear turned
to the earth, one to the wind in the trees.
How often I hear that song, even if
I never listen to it all the way through.

Owl

His territory is himself, his voles
and lizards, his ridgepoles, his eucalyptus.
For years, the same owl, the same hushed *huh-hu-*
hu-huu. But tonight, though he sits in the tree
outside the house, he seems to be calling
from a long way off, just as my age now

once was too far ahead to even call it
the future. No owl could be that old; yet
even owl song can reach the outer
stanza of what a self is, inquiring
of the night *huh-hu-who else?* And when
nobody counters in the language of owls

he goes on sounding out—how far to
the end of the street, the hill, the next
hill, the end of the sky and the end
of himself; and if no answer comes,
he negotiates with the silence. Then
it is so quiet I hear only distance.

Evening

The leaves falling from the plane trees
just before sunset take their places
in the classical formulary of light, and
after supper a girl climbs up to
the highest window in the house to look out.
Among the branches she can find neither
the body of Jesus nor anything else
that might be her life. The blue walls of clouds
crumble into snow. A dark lord has pried
reality open and descends through
the spinning flakes where I walked, once,
away from the arc lamps and the young men
who grew old leaning by the door
of the IGA. Now it is that evening.
Above the town a woman in the hills raises
her wine glass and says, *Let him keep my heart.*

The White Room

In the white room at the end of love
I saw again, after many years,
my girlfriend's sister in her bridal slip.
She was hurrying across the upstairs hall
to put on her makeup for the man
she would marry. I've forgotten how
it turned out for them, since the whiteness
of that room removes from itself any pettiness
or sorrow, and absolves us of the need
for an ending, happy or not. Seeing me,
she paused at the top of the stairs,
fussing an earring on, then smiled. A bell
elsewhere rhymed with something about
another time. She looked in that direction, said
sorry, but she really had to get ready.

II

Sorcerers

"Let's go," he said, "we have a long journey ahead of us."
—Carlos Castaneda

While Nixon bombed Hanoi, Allen took
my unread copy of *Journey to Ixtlan*
and studied it for weeks behind his closed door.
When I saw him again one day, he was sure
he'd mastered being in two places at once.

"Brother," I said, "as long as one of them isn't
Vietnam, show me the way!" We embraced
as only those apprenticed to belief embrace,
then drove Allen's Olds Eighty-Eight out into
the desert to train for the sorcerer's art.

The key to it was the gait of power. "Watch,"
Allen said as he leaned forward and began
shuffling his feet. He motioned for me to
copy him, and we began to jog in place,
lifting our knees high, our arms outstretched
to the horizon, our fingers raking up
some unseen substance—we looked
ridiculous. But I hoped it would work.

Suddenly Allen stopped. "Hey, man," he snapped,
as if he had heard my thoughts. "It's not
just Vietnam—the real war is *inside*—
got it?" "Got it," I replied. He started
tapping my chest. "If you can't stop your inner
dialogue, guess what? More war, more
loneliness, more of the ordinary."

Did I want that? I didn't want that.
I set off, jogging behind Allen,
bounding around the greasewood and mesquite
to remake myself as Carlos had to do
to become an artist of reality, that
pliant, misunderstood material.

True, at the moment I was the same tired
me I was always tired of, and beyond
the charisma of the invisible a hundred
B-52s executed their bombing runs.

But Allen *knew* he was onto something else,
and the longer I ran with him, dodging
cholla and prickly pear and the blades
of ocotillo, the bigger the sky got
in the late afternoon. And so I ran on,
towards the real thing, or the feeling of it.

The Great Wave off Kanagawa

She was stoned when she selected from
the artist's book a colored xerox of
Hokusai's block print—She liked that it showed
beauty is the source of its own peril.

The tattooist nodded; he'd heard that before.
She slept in the chair, her arm out to the side.
When she awoke there was no great wave,
no boats with boatmen ducking low,

just words that said in Japanese, *Thirty-Six
Views of Mount Fuji: The Great Wave off Kanagawa*.
The artist had misunderstood; to give her
the design of the original would have cost

a fortune. Yet he did a pretty job, inking
characters all along her inner arm, strange words
that looked a lot like the elaborate fins of
exotic fish in an aquarium, or birds flying

straight up to evade capture. Many years later,
holding her child high in her arms, she sees
as if from a watchtower men climbing into
a boat they will row out upon the waves.

We Hurried Onward

The guitar brings you back to me, the bass
notes sweep you away to the same place you
always end up going when that song plays.
Are you even alive? Of course you are.
Nobody dies when they're inside the sort of
music that made you drive through the night
with the headlights off. Maybe you hoped
the moon would erase you. But it didn't;
you're still glowing, unfastening your shirt
down to that last button, opening it wider
so I can slide my hands in and slip it
off your shoulders. Where else would life be
if not in you? Let me in, you said. Or did I?
A beautiful impurity, happening
and already over. How lightly we
said goodbye, then hurried onward as if
we would never wonder who we were.

My Dog the Artist

Sometimes I wish my dog had been an artist
so I'd have a keepsake besides the lock
of hair I snipped but then misplaced. Perhaps
I will still find it. Perhaps I would have
also lost the canvases inspired by
Brueghel or Chagall or Basquiat—
more likely Jackson Pollock, for Phineas
wasn't into narrative; he didn't
want to be in any story. Perhaps
he might have composed a touching piano
sonata for days when I miss him—sure,
it would have been for Dixie the beagle,
but I'd be okay with that. Or some
doggerel, payback for sleeping bored
under the desk and all the times, lost
in thoughts, I forgot him and an hour
later had to go back to the office
to let him out. How grumpy he looked sitting
on his side of the glass door as if to say
asshole. That's what I'd have said to me;
Phineas preferred defiance—like the time
I stopped for gas and left the key
inside the car and he stepped on the lock-out
button and pretended not to hear me
banging on the windows. Or the day we
moved, he went up our street to the next
street and downhill into the cool, little
dell to visit Herman the cocker
spaniel, biting me, after a two-
hour search, just hard enough to show me

as I carried him to the car that he
alone would be the judge of his gladness.
To that he was loyal, never backing down,
not to the Rottweiler that jumped the fence
or the pit bull that tore up his ribs.
Even in his final seizure he refused to die
until I made it home. Of course, as these things
with love go, he didn't leave me his oeuvre.
True to form he forced me to remember.

Burning Trash in Winter

Around the same time my parents were fed up
with my adolescence, the neighbors began to let
their dogs run loose. No matter what my father did—
heavy rocks on the lids, ropes through handles—
every night those dogs spilled the garbage cans.

So he bought a steel drum. He paid a man
to weld a hinged lid to the rim and put it
up on blocks near the edge of our lot.
Then, against my mother's objection,
he put me in charge of burning trash.

Discussions about my relationship with fire
soon followed: My mother had seen me
striking matches on my pants zipper, casting
one after the other like flower petals into
the milk cartons, the torn envelopes
scribbled over with totem poles of debt,
the old newspapers that concealed little
lamb bones or the crushed ribs of a chicken.

My mother began watching as she did
the dishes. To see me she had to lean past
her reflection in the kitchen window and wipe
the steam from the glass—was this the night
I'd set the old hen house on fire, spreading
flames into the neighbor's pine tree? She'd tilt
her head—was that the klaxon of the firemen?
The police coming to handcuff me to shame?

In the darkening days of a new decade
I perfected a new trick: Put two, four, six
matchsticks tip to tip, face them off like red-
masked wrestlers—jump back as the fire roared
towards the lowest limbs of the tree, close enough
to scare my mother into hammering the window.
I dropped the lid of the barrel. As fire does,
it settled its business with the world and died.
My parents sent me away to a boys' school.

I'd become a danger, said one. Danger*ous*,
corrected the other. The night before I left
I took out a last load of trash and, without
any sleight of hand, lit it on fire. Flames
leaped with icy joy, then matter-of-factly
vanished up the loose sleeve of night. I meant
to turn and go finish packing, but instead
plunged a hand through the hot ash, daring
the fire back. I was asking for it, as my
mother had warned, and the fire answered.

I brushed the ashes from my skin and watched
my hand shake. In time the Sixties would make
their own trash, and the fire would give us
the certainty of its sure reply. For now
the president was alive; what could I
do for my country but stand between
the bright kitchen window and the after-image
a small town makes as it recedes into
the horizon. A few dogs bark. Someone is calling
me to come in. It's evening, and cold.

Contre-Jour

War Zone C, Vietnam, 1966, *by Henri Huet: "The body of
an American paratrooper killed in action in the jungle near the
Cambodian border is lifted to an evacuation helicopter."*

The helicopter wallops the air; earthwards
the bamboos bend like fishing poles. You can
just make out the blossoms shadowing
the belly of the chopper towards which
the dead man, buoyed upon air, seems to rise
free of the caption below his body.
When you shoot against daylight—*contre-jour*—
everything is partially eclipsed by itself.
What Huet doubtless saw at first in the death
of a soldier was a kid again
launching a backflip in midair down at
the pond every boy remembers. But then
the evac takes away the photographic,
leaving only the light-sick eyes of
Henri Huet on his back, looking up.
He hated choppers. His own death would
circle him five more years. Then, on a hill
in Laos, daylight will catch the faces of
those about to kill him, another death
no one will ever see. In contre-jour,
light obscures to reveal. Huet saw it, didn't
need to look twice to know what was caught
between fact and heaven: the departure
of divinity, the boy-god flying
across time, nothing again, like the sky.

Could a Man Be a Snake?

Once, after she left New Pascua, Heather
told me that her ex-husband, the chief
of all the Yaquis, didn't need a phone to
receive word of his people on the Río Yaqui
in Sonora. He simply watched the ants.

She introduced me to him, at least in
his human form—because, Heather said, Anselmo
could shape-shift. The time I was cornered
by a rattler on Heather's patio
she came out and screamed for Anselmo to leave.
It was the *Sábado de Gloria*,
the Saturday after Christ's crucifixion,
also the day when the walls between
the living and the dead soften and yield to
the same wishes that commanded Jesus
to walk from the tomb. I went to Heather's.

So did the huge rattlesnake, in full
afternoon sun, hunting. Could a snake be
a man? The sound of the Easter rattles that shook
the square in New Pascua sent me up a ladder
onto Heather's roof. What was in the snake's
mind, if I believe her, was Anselmo,
warning her she could leave Yaqui but
it would never leave her alone. She'd always be
torn between two places. What can you do
with knowledge like that—either ignore it
or live as if a snake can be a man.

Heather heard me holler and came to the door.
There was the big snake blocking her way,
but when she saw who it was she hurled
curse after curse at Anselmo; Heather went
right up to the snake because they had
been in love once, but now it was over.

"Who knows?" Anselmo said to me before
I met him as a snake. "All kinds of change
is possible in the Creator's mind.
Nothing's ever finished. Even you.
Maybe you were one of us." He would ask
his dead mother the next time they talked.
She would know. He was sitting in the parlor
of an ordinary house, twirling some ice
in a glass. With outsiders he didn't have to be
a thousand percent Yaqui. He could take part
in the sister- and brotherhood of light
visible at night in the stars: the silver ants
of the Creator's mind, carrying back
and forth the work of endless reunion.

Red Shoes Floating on the Mekong

Wu-tsu said, "Sakyamuni and Maitreya are servants of another. Who is that other?"

The war is just another old story when
her boat skips the stop for sisters and princes,
and Cinderella steps to the prow

to answer the koan *Who Is That Other?*
She raises her arm and drops her pair of
brand-new red wedgies into the river.

They bump together, separate,
return, and finally abandon themselves
to the hospitality of the water.

Now there is no longer anyone those shoes
have to dance for; she hopes the river finds them
to be a perfect fit. She sails on, a guest

of the distance where the Mekong starts,
a guest of the moment that keeps slipping by
until there are no footprints left on the water.

Moonlight Sonata

Once they just stared from across the street.
Now nothing stops them, not even the new
medication. Which war is this? My sister
has lost track, but the soldiers keep coming,
slipping through the walls. Some lounge on sofas,
some open closets and drawers, inhaling her
favorite lovely things. A few stand by the bed
and watch her sleep, all of them deserters,
none of them willing to leave her. Each night
they promise they'll return to the front
as soon as the recital is over: They listen
with my sister to the beautiful
woman in white as she plays Beethoven
in the front yard—a vision of elegance,
my sister says, so much like our mother.
But nobody respects the past anymore.
The statuette of Venus lies in pieces
in the hall where the men gather to climb
the stairs. Whatever a mother's love was good for
is gone. Everything quakes in moonlight.
One child is spared. One is not.

Steve Orlen

Sunday, back in Tucson, doing yard work
at a small ranch in the desert, cutting
dead wood from the citrus, sycamores,
mesquites and pines, then raking out the leaves,
bark and branches, the neglect of many
seasons; and with me, but from above
the trees, is my friend Steve, his voice, his laugh,
his softly tremulous hands and head,
as if by shaking, despite his dread, he
also lived in perpetual assent. I
nod my head, too, as the work saws away
the hours and the clumsy uncomeliness
of the trees. What is no longer beautiful—
what to do with that? Chop, compost, spread it.

Above the trees we are free, even from
beauty. There is truth beneath the branches, but
that truth's been bent low by the truth sayers.
Who, then, to follow? Steve would say his
footsteps were too hard and heavy to walk
in, even for himself. On his arm
the bird tattoo, reminding him to sing
or, in lieu of song, fly above the words.
So he followed language and loved it,
and some of that shakes down on me today
as I rake up what the boughs discarded
and listen to Steve above the trees
where he says we don't have to talk anymore.

The Last Time I Saw Heather

The last time I saw Heather she was
walking ahead of me along a ridge
with a view from Baboquivari Peak
down to the Mexican border. Where better
to say goodbye than such a panorama?

But we weren't there for beauty. Beauty
was all around us, yet Heather's eyes
were casting about—when I caught up
she was crouching between two red rocks,
sifting through a pile of white powder.

I thought somebody had spilled a baggie
of drugs. I should have known they'd be
ashes she was raking over—with Heather,
where life and death met excited some
intelligence she had that I did not.

"Come look," she said, nodding at the powder
on the ground. "He's an old war vet biker."
She stopped pouring from one hand to another
and let the ashes settle thinly on her palm,
then pointed at some tiny, broken fetishes.

A girlfriend or wife had tossed them into
the cremation fire. She picked them out
and along her heart line set up a small, tarnished
circus made of a horse with no legs, half a snake,
a headless bear and a bird with one wing.

"That's you," she laughed. "But if you want to leave,
you'll need more than one wing." What will you need,
I was about to say, but didn't. She unslung her bag,
pulled out a cellophane envelope—inside,
two dead hummingbirds. They looked wrong there,

without a sky. She laughed at the face I made.
"What do you think we become when we die—
you'd rather be dust than love medicine? Here.
Take them. They'll carry love to you." I took
the birds; she dropped the broken charms into

her breast pocket, then clapped her hands. A puff
of ash drifted up. She looked straight at me, only
amusement in her eyes. She put her palms out
for me to find the smell of the old vet's life.
But he had no scent at all, except for hers.

Twilight

A hawk flies slow loops and eights, figures
of her reluctance to rest while the last light is
remembering whatever it touches. And then

from some nowhere of air a second hawk,
her mate, rises on circles to meet her
and together they glide over the hills

and disappear, not into our tallest woods,
but the inner world which also has trees
where hawks roost. There a boy is taking

his time to walk home. He's late, yet it's not
too dark to join a game of hide-and-seek.
He leans against a tree, counting by fives

when, just before he gets to *Ready or not*,
he sees in the pine needles by his feet
the same red-tail feather I keep here on my desk.

Beth in Summer

When I sit alone watching the waves yearn
for the shore, I don't think it's the Muse
pulling wool from my eyes. It's Beth. The moon
might tell me Beth is dead, but Beth has no age.
Like light she's mistaken for what she shines on.
So when I'm caught in the fall of waves and I
don't see her there, when the sun falls through trees
and I walk on, Beth understands: She walks on too,
in her summer dress, her belt gleaming like sleep,
buckling together the distance between the hum
of life and everything that has not happened
yet. Beth in white returning to the trees,
to the reluctance of the waves to break with
the past. Beth after each war, coming back from
the well of language, talking her way here again
to what life is. Simple as a sandwich
and a sweet pickle. Or a handsome man
in a wide-brimmed hat. Or the night sliding
into her arms as she walks among us listening for
the words she came to hear: *Don't leave me.*

Stroudsburg

What was I—twelve?—when the Civil Defense
sirens collapsed the roof timbers of
childhood and the Communist fireball soon
would suck up every man, woman and child
and roar through our towns with laughter.
I slid under my bed and saw in the dustballs
the precursors of my fate. Three minutes left
to live, and what to do with them? I looked
around. A blue cat's-eye. A packet of
grape Lik-m-aid, the top torn off—in my
short life I'd had a sweet tooth. A pair of
BVDs, a fond memento of sex with
myself which, it was my impression, was
practice for the girl I would now never meet
and in whose arms I was not destined to die.
A pencil stub from an earlier age and near it
a Sinclair road map of Pennsylvania,
dear neighboring state where I would
never venture in a white Mercury
convertible with custom red leather seats
and the same girl I would not make love with
sitting next to me, a scarf over her hair.
The last thing I ever saw, before
the radiation melted all the soft
parts of her I knew nothing about,
was that look of gratitude for taking her
with me to Pennsylvania. O
Pennsylvania! Thank you for being
there as we drove in no particular order
through Pittsburgh and Edensburg, Harrisburg,

Gettysburg and many other burgs until
at one-o-three the all clear pushed air back
into my lungs and so: life. In which I soon
forgot I had died and gone to
Pennsylvania where the news was Ricky
Flatte's father had also gone, living in
sin in Stroudsburg with a fallen woman.

My City

It may not really be my city—just
what I think is there, across a macramé
of street lights people like me are
knotted to, some of us in worry awake,
or gone from the dream to the kitchen,
some clenched or purified by childhood scenes,
or saved by luck or ruined by it, driving around
kicking up leaves and candy wrappers,
all of us in the dark along our own
coastlines of doubt. I should be asleep, too,
but I came to the door to see my city
lit up in tentative kindness. In case
it vanishes, here I am, up early,
perhaps too early, or did I come too late?
The first bird, the last bird, is not in the sky.

The Hammock

How did we ever get a hammock? Possibly
it was to please my mother, but more likely
a feeling came over my father out in
the country where he sold people things
they really didn't want. In their faces
he saw their ambivalence about whether
they distrusted him or themselves. But
on the way back from *the road*, as he called
selling, for a short time all around him
in the canopies of trees that bordered streams
he saw an unending welcome, or in
the lettuce fields of black dirt an invitation
to stay and just look, or sit forever beneath
the big cowherds of clouds over Allamuchy
and Succasunna, towns whose strange and
unlikely names made him think of the soul.

And yet *soul* was never a word that crossed
my father's lips. It didn't tie in with
anything, unlike the hammock he bought
in Dover at the Army Navy store, the kind
you hang between posts or trees. But we
had no trees growing close together;
my father hadn't thought of where
the second anchor could be. Another tree,
a post, the past—what could he connect to?
He left the hammock in the grass to be
flecked with raindrops and the footprints of birds.

My mother, too, was silent about the soul;
best to leave that hidden, like the orioles' nest

we knew must be there but had never seen.
For weeks the hammock lay in the grass;
one evening I sat down on the canvas
and rolled side to side as if *I* were the hammock—
the colored clouds and all that blue moved like
a lady's paper fan, faster and faster.
I got dizzy watching how easy it was
for one thing to become another thing.
My mother laughed; we picked up the hammock,
brushed off the grass, and carried it to the porch.
From chains hooked to the rafters she hung it—
my mother had a plan: she'd already
painted the porch ceiling blue. She got in
and settled upon the current of that
late August night. "Where are you going?"
I asked. "Oh you tell me," she said, more tired
than interested. "Dover High School."
"No! Not there, please," because soon that's where she
would be all day, teaching the sophomore girls.
"Silly," she murmured, then was soon asleep.

Out the hammock went as I pushed, then it
brought her back. Out and back. Out to the future,
which would not be kind to her, then back
where the failing light changed the shape of her nose,
her hair that in the dark looked darker. Her lips,
her head slipped to the side towards the night—
I was a child in the sway of the music of
the hammock, the swung music of breath
and creaking rope, the high hum of the chains,
the drum-thump of canvas against my hands and

the swish of her soul, as I pushed my mother away
and received her back into my hands again,
and again pushed her away, as I do now.

Peonies

Those robust peonies floated a day
or two in a green vase across the room,
red flotsam of life's high tide. Night by night
that red has been retreating to rose,
pink, pearl. Just before peonies die
they lose all color—except an edgy
ghost of red, like lipstick that didn't
come off before bed. Today we wake early,
restless. Remember how when love was new
it hedged itself with disbelief? We had
so many last days the last day never came.
Now the peonies are as pale as white can be,
their petals glowing with completion.

The Beauty of You

I'm not that fussy about where to die.
I'd be happy with the woods on the high side
of a road with no shoulders and some
S-curves to please my fondness for speed.
Spring in mountains, maybe near a stream
running so fast it scatters stones in its way.
That kind of speed. A quickening. Also
some altitude, so the spirit is readily
teased into updrafts. That would do it,
a beauty sufficient enough to call it
Nature, yet familiar enough to also
call it *you*. As I die, I'll hear my voice
and think, Wait a second, that's not
me. That's the wind calling—or is it
you? *Yes*, I'll answer out of habit, *what
is it, honey?* I'll wonder, Uh-oh, did I
leave a wet towel on the floor or forget
to empty the dishwasher? As if my death
might really be nothing more than another
domestic chore, hardly life's lonely end.
For what is this I, this me, without you
to whom I speak even when I'm just
talking to myself? And maybe it will be
only the wind asking you on that day
to keep all of me with you that you can.

The Apology

That it was his nurse for whom our doctor
had left his wife I was vaguely aware,
and as well that she was, in Dad's sex-whispered
word, *buxom*, the relevance of which was
tempered by my mother's revulsion at men
who were interested in one thing and one
thing only. But some *thing* must have happened;
the nurse-wife abruptly left him; I never knew
the whole story. Paul returned to living
with his first wife, my mother's friend. Years passed;
right after my father died, Paul came over.
He hadn't aged well. I offered to take his coat.
No, he said, he could not stay, nor could he attend
the service. He'd come to pay his respects.

He was sorry, he said, for my loss which
he too felt: the loss of an old friend. . . .
To my mother he said he was sorry that
he had to be in Livingston at his lawyer's;
he had invented a machine for cleansing
the blood and was applying for a patent.
In his heavy coat he walked to the far end
of the kitchen and took a chair across from
my mother and started to say something
that began with her name and ended with
lust has left my loins. That was how he put it.

He sat bowed before her. Perhaps I was
more stunned than my mother. I stood at a distance,
a space that was suddenly there like the cliff

at the end of the past where the dreamer
finally knows everything too late—
in the icy silence of her response, the words
lust has left my loins actually seemed to twinkle
like the small diamonds of an atonement.

But my mother would give Paul nothing, not
a thank-you, not a touch of the hand, and Paul
saw he had not offered enough. There were
tears in his eyes as he fixed his hat
against the cold outside, nodded to me,
then with difficulty shuffled across
the slippery drive. My mother sat there
looking at him from the same chair that
a week before had been my father's.
Paul's car turned at the corner; my mother
went on looking, looking for the ghost who
would give her the apology she deserved.

Two Cherries

Before we knew if you would live
we took a trip to France, and in every
cathedral town in Saône-et-Loire and Côte d'Or
we lit candles. Don't tell a soul, you said
each time, Jewish girl with a Catholic heart.
On Pont Marie you fought back tears—
the Parisian light thick as lemon conserve
in the plane trees, the accordions pumping
Histoire d'un amour as the boats sailed the Seine.

Maybe the last time, Paris. . . . On Louis-Philippe
we bought two blue-checkered cups for luck,
at the bottom of each, a pair of cherries.
And you lived; it was not expected.

Now I look out the window, holding my cup.
I watch you walk the dog, dressed for work,
your brown curls shining, the dog sniffing
the year's new jasmine. An angel might
appear, lost in the wrong century.
But I don't look for angels. Just us.
At the bottom of the cup, two cherries
not quite touching, and that little space
between them that makes love possible.

Autumn

At his birth in autumn my brother was
turned back, unnamed, which does not

mean he ever left, but, like a wizard
from thin air, he used for his blood

the sap of a hollow tree, assigning
to the season all the yellow his leaves

would need, and to me a box of pencils
containing the past he'd been denied,

and a rake, his way of saying
the work of families is never done.

My Angel in Winter

They say you can't see an angel until you've
seen your sorrow. I've never asked him if
that's true, but I do see my angel each time
I get back in bed after maybe the third pee
of the night. How tired he looks from
a lifetime of watching over me, his slovenly
garment hanging on him like a laundry bag
someone stuffed an angel into. Time spent in
time has sallowed his skin, dried it. If I were he
I'd always be turning my face to heaven,
asking the rain to fall as holy exfoliant.
But that's not my angel's style. He's a complete
pro. He never even takes the side of
the angels on the question of mortality.
He's here solely to console the past. Of course
when I close my eyes I know he'll be there
when I wake up. But is that the same as
being there for me? More and more I sense
his ambiguity as he rises from his chair
by the window to feel the breeze that makes
the curtains flutter, or stands with his back
to me, gazing at my unfinished city,
listening to the lamentations of traffic.

Elegy for Photography

"Entrée du passage de la Réunion, 1 et 3 Rue du Maure, 3°," 1911
by Eugène Atget

In Atget's shot of the forge in *le passage
de la Réunion*, the metalsmith poses
behind the gate of his small factory,
bare armed, tongs resting on the edge of
the cooling bath. Have you a wife? Atget asks;
yes he does, upstairs. Call her to the window.
The woman comes, but so petite! And
the camera is already set in place—
to see her at all Atget must ask Madame
to please stand on the window ledge. Small but
plucky, up she goes, balances there—
ready to risk a fall for photography.
Ne bougez pas, Atget warns, and, lifting
the black drape of his art, disappears.

The woman sees a man half in the shawl
of the graveyard; Atget frames the scene, thinks
real life's become an antiquity. Yet there
in the narrow passage is a small surprise:
a boy the size of punctuation peeking
around the corner—*Qu'est-ce qui se passe?*
But it's not up to Atget to explain
what's going on. He packs up his gear,
says *bonne journée* and heads off to his next
lost cause. Behind the gate the smithy
stokes the fire, his wife pulls the shutters in.
And the boy? He goes where boys will go,
down a street we can no longer see into.

The Old Songs

At the end of her life, my sister searched
for meaning. She found instead a large white
egg made of sugar with pink stripes
piped around it, and at one end a peephole
through which she saw a beautiful lake,
and behind that, in the distance, a tall mountain.

Although she was ill and not able
to walk far, she went inside the egg
and followed the path above the water.

How pleasant to amble across such a grand
place in nature! In no time at all she reached
the big blue mountain with its tall blue door.
She opened it—a short hallway led right into
a room in the sky where a large squirrel
was waiting. "Ah, glad you made it," he said.

"What is this," my sister asked, "the threshold
of some kind of rebirth? Because if it is,
that's not what I came for." "Well, what were you
expecting," he said, a bemused look on his face,
"Albert Schweitzer?" "Yes!" my sister said.

"How did you know?" As a girl she had
practically worshipped the doctor; in her eyes
he stood above all others—if she could not
find meaning, then she wanted such a man to
admire. "But—is all I get you?" she asked.

The squirrel smiled. "Oh I hear that quite often
these days. People have such strange ideas

about life, as if they had some kind of
claim on it. Shall we?" the squirrel said.
My sister slipped her arm in his,
and as they left he sang to her in a fine
baritone the old songs of sorrow's end.

The Snow One Night

Before I knew what woke me up I walked
across the dark to the bedroom window.

From there I could just make out someone slowly
turning, dervish-like, in the heavy snow.

Who are you? I said, fogging the glass
with my breath. I drew another window

on the windowpane and looked through it;
the man in the yard below looked straight back.

It was my father in slippers and pajamas,
his hair filled with snowflakes, his arms reaching

towards something beyond our yard. What
did he see that I could not? Whatever it was

made him happy because he gave that
two-fingered salute which always meant

he was feeling good. And so my father
spun on, twirling in and out of evidence

until what was left of him and his dance
was a phantom arm, a hand upturned, then

just snow. And the snow went on falling harder
and faster, past the shooting stars and planets

a boy at a window once drew across
the invisible history of the night.

Pure Lloyd

Before the hurricane ended our vacation,
Lloyd would get up early and walk far down
the beach to his morning rendezvous with
the Miniature Man, a stranger I never met
whose passion was the smallest, most beautiful
seashells. By the time the rest of us got up,
Lloyd would be at the sink gently washing
each shell. He liked to set them out
on the table at breakfast, near his egg whites
with tabasco, and watch our reactions,
adding simply, "I met the Miniature Man."

The minuscule shells—cowries, stars, tulips,
wings, hearts—would pass from hand to hand.
Never very many, five or ten a day, shells
we supposed were chosen by the Miniature Man,
pale silver and pink, shades especially
poignant in that morning light. As we turned
each one over, we could see where
a tiny animal had lived like a child
facing the bedroom wall, or a genie who
foretold in shades of silver and dark blue
the biggest storm in a century. We fled just as
the flood came, and left behind Lloyd's box of shells.

"Who was the Miniature Man?"
I asked Lloyd years later, when he was dying.
Lloyd claimed he couldn't remember. "Was he
a small man from Ohio?" That was Lloyd,
to distract with a joke and never let on

where he was getting his information.
Towards the end we were holding hands.
Lloyd looked at them intertwined. Was this
my idea of a date? Then he sank back
into the pillow and said it was weird
to no longer be thirsty—he was done with
water. He'd left the glass by his bed.

He wanted me to see that little detail,
the unfinished glass of water—meaning,
if I understand him right, neither
the glass half-empty nor half-full but
the glass, the shell around this tender life
which so easily flows away. He meant:
When your heart ceases to beat the oceans
don't stop, and neither does the ocean
in your heart. Sounds incredible, doesn't it?

But that's what Lloyd says as we walk
along the water of the Miniature Man's mind,
me bare headed, Lloyd in his zinc oxide
and crumpled hat, the two of us bending
at exactly the same moment to lift a tiny
bivalve the way the Miniature Man instructed,
holding it just so, as you would a stranded
seraphim whose pale blue wings are covered
with sand. That was Lloyd, Lloyd and his secrets,
Pure Lloyd, always showing me what to look for.

My Swedish Son

The son I never had is standing on
the edge of the deck in a white shirt,
his wide back to the house where I watch him

from behind a curtain, curious
about this strange love child. *Jag will hora
lite musik*—I want to hear some music

he says, leaning over a railing,
taking in the city. *Det ar mycket warmt har*—
it's very warm here. *Hur lange varar den?*

How long does it last? How long does anything
last, I sigh, puzzled by my Swedish son.
I'm wondering if maybe a trip up the coast

would be good for him, and me. . . . In this age
of estrangement, too much distance between
father and son is bad for the family.

But why don't I remember his mother?
Should I say something? Before I can ask
he says, *Kan ni dansa samba?* Ah, he's

warming up to me. No, I cannot samba,
not with this trick hip. But your mother,
now there was a woman who could dance!

My Father's Last Address Book

Rose knew his cheapness well, so she bought
the Woolworth's address book refill, two pages
per letter of the alphabet, good enough
for a dying business. She taped up
the spine of the old cover with its gold
coconut palm, and slipped the refill in.
Under each letter she wrote some contacts,
perfectly alphabetized, to give him
the idea— Arctic Cooling, Dover Trust,
Joe this, Larry that, Tap-Rite Products— each
entry inscribed in blue-black script with big-
bosomed capitals and vowels which
folded like secrets over themselves.

At first my father seems to have grasped
the value of order, although maybe not
the subtleties of the pen whose owner
under R wrote her name in crimson.
He gave it a try: American Vending,
Atlantis Cargo, but already at B
Red Lobster crept in; under D, Peerless Gas;
at P, a note to himself: *Send Simmons 4.*

Rose was my father's alphabet; she spent
more time with him than any of us did,
day after day from the 1950s
until he closed his business.
I remember her as polite, but guarded,
only slightly friendly. A black pen stood
like a warning at the front of her desk.

She was pretty when young, and older as well,
but prettiness visibly saddened.

Shortly after his death Rose also died.
"*See?*" my mother said, pointing to Rose's
place in the local notices of deaths,
"*They practically died in bed together!*"
My father was too careful a man for that;
he left us little of what you'd call
his truest self. So I looked for him in
the address book, and for Rose. But I'm not
sure what I found—doodles, darts and names—
it all flared out like Roman candles between
torn-apart clouds of half-erased addresses.

At XYZ, the last name she put in
was *Zimmer,* not in blue ink but pencil,
with an arrow and circled phone number.
That was all I found—until I started again
at A and read under C in Rose's hand
Dr. Zimmer—my father had been diagnosed
with cancer; she must have known and
did not think what page to put it on.
When he called me all he said was he had to
start radiation soon; he was fine, but
he wanted time alone first, to sort things out.

Where he went I never knew. Maybe
Allamuchy, Barnegat Light, Cape May,
the places nearby he had loved. Maybe the far

islands whose romance costs more than
the alphabet. He came back, sold the business,
finished his treatments and died a year later.

For the rest of her life my mother
believed in betrayal. "*I knew it*,"
she insisted. "*I knew it!*" "No," I said,
"no, you didn't know." That's all I told her.
But I hoped he went with Rose somewhere,
even if it wasn't true. He seems always
to have been under the spell of address
unknown. Would Rose have put his life
in order? She waited for him beneath
the gold palm tree as long as she could.

Pilgrim at Thoor Ballylee, 1969

I got off the bus at Gort and walked the last
miles along many wet, nearly spiritual,
little roads to Thoor Ballylee. It was closed.
But I met the nice lady who had the key
and invited me in to have a look around,
to climb up and down the actual
winding stairs of W. B. Yeats—What was
the great Yeats like? I asked my patient host.
Tall, he was tall. Ah. And did he build
the tower? Yeats? Oh no, not Yeats.

Yeats never did a stitch of work. Oh, I said,
and asked, might I then take her photo? No, please;
but you'll want one of that, she said, pointing
to the stone set to the front of the tower
right above the road, Yeats' strange, dark wish:

> And may these characters remain
> When all is ruin once again.

—But who'd be around to read in the ruins?
All in all, I thought, poem and tower
a bit of a letdown, except from the roof.

There the clouds had the look of revelations
kicked up by horsemen, the Irish flag burning
green and orange amongst them. So I walked back
along the ordinary road a little hopeful
and thought as I went to the nowhere
I came from, If there is a soul, it must be
like the stream running past Thoor Ballylee

through the descending dark, or the memory of it,
to be somewhere it already is.

The New Year

for Susan

The same sun again setting in the middle
of the present. Six or seven ravens
circling, climbing towards the high hills.
Another evening is the only evening
to them as well, and as they always do,
right above the house the stragglers turn
and wheel around the roof a time or two,
tugged by the string of a clock made of feathers,
and when they're gone, here comes the red
helicopter, stuttering west into a headdress
of twilight. Come out and see this—an entire
year is passing like thread through the eye
of the last day of the year. Close the mystery
book—in the end, Lieutenant Lugubrious
restores order to Labrador. Come out
and sit beside me with the birds and stones
at the purple edge of our life together.
I'm not looking for anything that
isn't already here, except you.

The Ghost of Phineas

Remember when I lay by your feet
beneath the desk? I'd wonder: How can he
be so slow? You never had an answer,

yet I still hoped for whatever happens next,
some afterwards of sleep where there's a sky
beyond each sentence. Now you look up,

searching the air for another word for
air. *Phineas* would be my suggestion.
So much simpler to have one word for

everything. Phineas—yes, that works.
Isn't it me you've called to come in out of
the blue? Me, your ghost dog who always

preferred being somewhere close. True, a ghost
can run wild. Although what I do now, let's not
call it running. I circulate at the will or

whim of a brilliance you'd think could hold
a ghost together long enough for you
to see me. Instead, after I died patience

became my art: I go on watching and
waiting, still worried I left before you came
to the right ending. How would you find it?

Look up more often. Maybe linger
by a window. Or, best of all, just walk
out the door into the old sameness

of hills and hellos where our pleasure
was big enough to save even
the worst day. Go ahead. Go out.

Look—isn't that a small bird fallen down
on the side of the road? Yes, I believe so.
Everyone has passed by, except you.

What happens next? I'll tell you: When you
reach down she opens her eyes and flies off,
bright and green as the leaves where I leave you.

My Parents in the City of Light

After they died, they arrived in Paris.
They had always wanted to see the sights,
but there was only enough time to seek out
a distant relative of ours in one of
the outer arrondissements. Monsieur Dumont
(that was his name) was unsurprised to see them,
since he expected such visits from obscure
kin like my parents, who came before him with
their last rays of selfhood. My parents had heard
he was skilled at correcting the past; *non*,
M. Dumont said in very simple French,
this was beyond what a mere *bricoleur*
like him was allowed; for this, they needed
someone more skilled than a handyman.
What M. Dumont could do was help them
vacate the space which they were so
accustomed to they couldn't see that they'd
left it filled with disappointment. He explained
why we expect more from life than we receive,
and why, to give itself, life needs more than
just our one body, or our little world—but here
he saw his guests didn't really understand.
So he tried to say it again as best he could
in English. My parents nodded as if they had
suspected as much, but M. Dumont spoke
with such a heavy accent they hadn't
grasped a word he said. They sat for a while
in that tiny front room holding hands
before they let go of each other and became
part of a knowledge we imagine some day
finding in a book, a city, or a face we love.

Photos referenced from "Contre-Jour" and "Elegy for Photography" follow with their permissions:

"The body of an American paratrooper killed in action in the jungle near the Cambodian border is lifted to an evacuation helicopter," 1966. AP Photo/Henri Huet. Used by permission of Associated Press.

Eugène Atget, 1911: Entrée du passage de la Réunion, 1 et 3 Rue du Maure, 3° arrondissement. Digital image courtesy of Getty's Open Content Program.

I want to thank Lawrence Raab, Kathleen Flenniken, John Mottishaw and Peter Persic for their friendship and generous readings, conversations, and suggestions. Thanks to Alex Kivowitz, Betsy Anderson, Hilma Wolitzer and Brenda Hillman for their early encouragement during my return to poetry. My thanks to Philip Perkis for the lessons in cameras, seeing and being, and to Susan Kent whose light is everywhere in these poems.